OCTOPUSES

by Colleen Kessler

Content Consultant
John A. Cigliano
Department of Biological Sciences
Cedar Crest College

CORE
LIBRARY

Published by ABDO Publishing Company, PO Box 398166, Minneapolis, MN 55439. Copyright © 2014 by Abdo Consulting Group, Inc. International copyrights reserved in all countries. No part of this book may be reproduced in any form without written permission from the publisher. The Core Library™ is a trademark and logo of ABDO Publishing Company.

Printed in the United States of America,
North Mankato, Minnesota
102013
012014

Editor: Mirella Miller
Series Designer: Becky Daum

Library of Congress Cataloging-in-Publication Data
Kessler, Colleen.
  Octopuses / by Colleen Kessler.
      pages cm. -- (The smartest animals)
  Includes bibliographical references and index.
  ISBN 978-1-62403-169-4
1. Octopuses--Juvenile literature. I. Title.
QL430.3.O2K47 2014
594'.56--dc23
                          2013029176

Photo Credits: Richard Whitcombe/Shutterstock Images, cover, 1; Tips Images/SuperStock, 4; iStockphoto/Thinkstock, 7, 26; Dave Fleetham/Pacific Stock-Design Pics/SuperStock, 9, 38, 43; John Woodcock/DK Images, 11; Minden Pictures/SuperStock, 12, 15; Universal Images Group/SuperStock, 16, 45; Rostislav Ageev/Shutterstock Images, 18; Hemera/Thinkstock, 21; Hal Beral VWPics/SuperStock, 22; Red Line Editorial, 28; David Evison/Shutterstock Images, 31; Biosphoto/SuperStock, 32; Norbert Probst/imagebroker.net/SuperStock, 34; Rich Carey/Shutterstock Images, 41

CONTENTS

CHAPTER ONE

ALL ABOUT OCTOPUSES

February 26, 2009, was an eventful morning at the Santa Monica Pier Aquarium in California. Aaron Kind was the first staff member to arrive for work. He was shocked to find the aquarium flooded with approximately 200 gallons (757 L) of water. Kind checked the tank. A one-foot (0.3-m) long two-spotted octopus was swimming in what little water was left in the tank. The octopus had taken apart a

Octopuses are super-smart animals that live throughout our world's oceans.

valve at the top of the tank. The octopus could have been trying to escape. Or it could have been curious about the valve. This valve controlled the flow of water. Water had already sprayed from the tank for more than 10 hours by the time Kind arrived.

Aquarium specialist Nick Fash created a system to prevent the valve from being removed again. But octopuses are known for their intelligence. Even with Fash's changes, there was a chance the octopus would figure out how to take apart the valve again.

Soft-Bodied Invertebrates

Octopuses are cephalopods. A

What Are Cephalopods?

Cephalopods include squid, cuttlefish, nautiluses, and octopuses. They are found in oceans. Cephalopods live close to shore and also in very deep areas of the ocean. Most cephalopods hide when in danger. Some do this by squirting a cloud of ink and moving quickly away. Cephalopods are among the most intelligent invertebrates. They have highly advanced senses of smell, touch, and sight.

Many octopuses live near small spaces. These areas make for good homes and hiding places.

cephalopod is a kind of mollusk. Cephalopods have a head with eyes and a brain. They also have a set of arms or tentacles. Some cephalopods shoot black ink out of their bodies when in danger. Others are able to create a cloud of light.

Cephalopods are invertebrates. This means they do not have a spine. There are more than 200 species of octopuses found in all of Earth's oceans. They often swim in shallow waters up to depths of three miles (5 km). Octopuses live in rocky coastal areas or coral reefs. They also live in open ocean waters and sandy areas.

Octopus species range in size from 1 inch (2.5 cm) to 16 feet (5 m) long. Male octopuses are usually smaller than females. The giant Pacific octopus is the largest species. These large octopuses can weigh up to 110 pounds (50 kg). No matter their size, octopuses are strong. They can be defensive if they sense danger. Some octopuses carry venom in their bodies. The blue-ringed octopus is one of these species. It uses its venom when attacking prey or when it is being attacked.

An octopus's head is between its eyes. The head holds the animal's brain and beak. An octopus also has a sac near the head called the mantle. The mantle contains all of an octopus's organs, including three hearts. An octopus's entire body is soft except for the hard beak. Octopuses do not have any bones. This helps octopuses hide in very small spaces.

An octopus's eight arms help it survive.

Amazing Arms

An octopus's eight arms branch directly from the head. These arms are very strong and bendable. Octopuses can move their arms in any direction since they do not have any bones. Octopuses use their arms for eating, moving, hunting, and mating. The arms contain most of the nerves in an octopus's body.

Most octopus species have two rows of suckers on each arm. The common octopus has approximately 240 suckers on each arm. These suckers are very sensitive. They grab onto prey. Suckers can also determine the texture, shape, and taste of whatever they are touching. Tiny receptors on the suckers pick up the features of an object. Then the receptors send a message to the octopus's brain. The brain then determines what the object is.

Seeing, Breathing, and Moving

Octopuses have great vision. They can tell the size, shape, and brightness of things from far away. But they cannot see in color.

Octopuses breathe through gills. The gills pull oxygen from the water. The water is pushed out

---

Three Hearts

Octopus blood carries oxygen throughout their bodies, like human blood. But octopus blood is not as good as human blood at moving the oxygen throughout the body. Octopuses have three hearts to help move the oxygen. Two hearts pump blood through the gills. The third heart moves the oxygen-rich blood throughout the body.

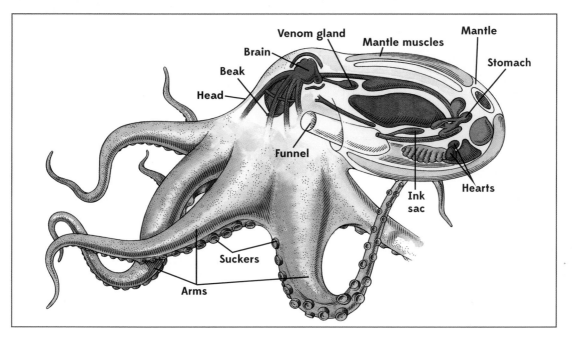

Octopus Features

Octopuses have many features and each part serves a special purpose. This diagram shows where some main body features are located on an octopus. How might some of these parts help an octopus survive?

through a flexible funnel near the eyes. The oxygen is circulated throughout the body.

The suckers on an octopus's arms help it move along the ocean floor. If an octopus needs to move more quickly, it can push water through its funnel.

CHAPTER TWO

THE SHORT LIFE OF AN OCTOPUS

Octopuses have a short lifespan. Most octopuses live approximately one year. Some species of octopus can live up to five years. Octopuses are considered adults when they are ready to mate. This age varies among species. Some females begin looking for a mate when they are between three and five years old. Other species with shorter lifespans

Most octopus species have short lifespans, living no more than five years.

begin looking even earlier. Octopuses live alone until they are ready to mate.

Caring for the Eggs

Male and female octopuses do not stick together after mating. Some female octopuses have even been known to eat their male mates after mating. A female holds the eggs inside of her until she is ready to lay them. Sometimes she mates with several males. Most octopus species will only lay eggs once in its lifetime.

Female octopuses lay between 50 and 100,000 eggs in shelters under rocks or in holes. The number of eggs depends on the species. Laying eggs can take a few weeks. One by one, the

Amazing Argonauts

The argonaut is an octopus found in tropical and semi-tropical waters. The female grows to be approximately four inches (10 cm) long. The male only grows to be approximately one inch (2 cm) long. A female argonaut may lay eggs multiple times throughout her life. This is different than most octopus species.

Female octopuses are protective of their eggs until they hatch. But baby octopuses must take care of themselves after hatching.

female glues each egg to the walls and ceiling of the nest so they do not wash away. Some females attach the eggs in hanging clusters. Some clusters have up to 1,000 tiny eggs.

The female protects her eggs until they hatch. She keeps predators away by blocking the entrance to the shelter. She usually will not eat during the 2 to 14 months it takes for her eggs to hatch. The amount

Octopuses grow quickly since many octopus species have short lifespans.

of time depends on the species and the water temperature. The female octopus keeps the eggs clean by moving water currents across them.

Most female octopuses die after their eggs hatch. Male octopuses also die within months of mating. However, by laying so many eggs, octopuses produce a lot of offspring quickly. This helps keep the species alive and growing.

Newborn Drifters

Newborn octopuses have no parental care once they are born. Most newborn species cannot swim and rely on water currents to move them. Other octopus species can move like adults right after hatching.

Newborn octopuses grow quickly. Some double in size every week.

Scientists know very little about the early life of octopuses. In approximately 50 percent of species, newborns spend time living among plankton. Then they will spread out from one another across the ocean floor. The other 50 percent of species make lairs immediately. They look for caves, holes, and other types of shelter near the ocean floor to call home. They hide in these lairs and other small spaces. From there, they prey on crab, crayfish, clams, lobsters, fish, and other mollusks. Octopuses catch these animals with their arms. Then they bite the prey and inject it with venom to kill it before eating it.

Hunting for Prey

When fish, shrimp, lobster, or other food swims by, the octopus reaches out with an arm. The octopus stops its prey with its suckers. It then injects it with venom. If the prey has a hard shell, the octopus crunches through it with its strong beak.

CHAPTER THREE

INTELLIGENT OCTOPUSES

Scientists believe octopuses are among the smartest invertebrates on Earth. It is hard to tell exactly how smart they are, though. An octopus's brain is much different than other animals. Unlike most other animals, including humans, the majority of an octopus's nerves are found throughout its body, not in the brain. Octopuses gather information by touching objects. This makes octopus

Octopuses can be hard to find, which can make research challenging.

intelligence difficult to measure. Octopuses can also be hard to find in the ocean. In comparison to many animals, scientists know little about many octopus species.

Thieves in the Night

Octopuses can be very tricky. Scientists often set bait boxes in the ocean to attract marine life to document or study. It does not take long for local octopuses to discover the food. The octopuses work hard to pick the lock and steal the bait. In one video taken off the coast of South Africa, an octopus gets through several zip ties and steals the entire bait box. Even more impressive, the octopus stole the box while being attacked by a shark.

Signs of Intelligence

Octopuses are known for being very clever. For years, fishers have reported octopuses stealing fish and lobsters from their traps and nets. Octopuses can slide through the holes of the traps. Once inside, octopuses help themselves to the fisher's catch.

Some scientists believe octopus

An octopus's arms have more nerve endings than the rest of its body.

intelligence is due in part to the size of their brains. Octopus brains are the largest for their body size among invertebrates.

Smart Behaviors

The true signs of octopus intelligence are behavior-related. Scientists have observed octopuses in the wild and in captivity. They do amazing things in both habitats. Octopuses have been observed playing with

Veined octopuses are known for using empty coconut shells as shelters.

balls and empty plastic bottles in aquariums. Some octopuses were observed using their funnel to shoot water at objects. This pushed the animals away from the object so they could reach out to recover it. It appeared as if the octopuses were playing fetch with themselves.

Octopuses in the wild have been seen using tools. The veined octopus collects empty coconut shells. It pulls the shell under its body and walks back to where it plans to build its lair. The octopus uses the shells as lumber to build its lair. Other species of octopuses have been seen collecting rocks. They pile the rocks in front of their lairs overnight. This keeps them safe from predators as they sleep.

Octopuses have another clever way to protect themselves from predators. They can detach one of their arms when they are attacked. Hopefully the predator will focus on the arm, allowing the octopus to escape. An octopus may also purposely lose an arm if it is trying to fit into a small space. An octopus is able to regrow any lost arms. Scientists are unsure how long it takes for a new arm to grow.

Inking the Ocean

Many cephalopods, including octopuses, can shoot black ink out of their bodies when they feel they are in danger. The ink confuses predators and allows the octopus time to swim away. The ink sac is near the digestive gland. Depending on the species, some octopuses can shoot ink in different forms. Some squirt a blob that leaves an octopus-like shape to confuse their predators.

Solving Problems

Octopuses also show their intelligence by solving problems. When scientists give an octopus a plastic bottle with a crab inside, the octopus will work to get to its prey. The octopus tries to force the jar open as if it is a clam or mussel. The octopus will eventually discover how to unscrew the bottle top.

Octopuses learn from their problem-solving attempts too. Once they learn how to open something, they will remember for the next time.

John Blaine wrote a science-adventure story titled *The Wailing Octopus* in 1956. This excerpt shows Rick and Scotty, the main characters' interest in learning more about octopuses as they scuba dive:

> *Directly ahead was a small shelf. Rick moved to Scotty's side and saw the dark opening of a cave. Next to the opening was a small octopus. As they approached he changed color, trying to imitate the multicolored coral against which he rested.*
>
> *Rick reached out a hand and the animal retreated, sliding into the mouth of the cave. Apparently this was his home, because the ledge was littered with shells from a number of meals.*
>
> Source: John Blaine. The Wailing Octopus. *New York: Grosset & Dunlap, 1956. Print.*

What's the Big Idea?

Take a close look at Blaine's words. Remember his work is fiction. What is Blaine's main idea? What evidence is used to support his point? Come up with a few sentences showing how Rick and Scotty use two or three pieces of evidence to support Blaine's main point.

CHAPTER FOUR

DANGER AND DEFENSE

Octopuses live in every ocean. They can only survive in salt water. Octopus species live in different habitats. These include rocky coastal areas, reefs, the ocean floor, and sandy areas. Their favorite habitat is any spot with a lot of prey and hiding places. Octopuses hide in tiny cracks and crevices.

Coral reefs are good places for octopuses to find prey. Reefs also offer many hiding places for octopuses.

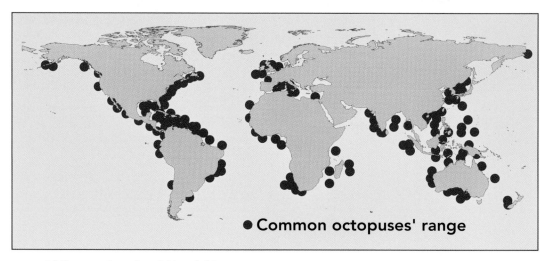

● Common octopuses' range

Where in the World?

This map shows the worldwide distribution of the common octopus, the most-studied octopus species. As you can see, the common octopus can be found along most of the world's coasts. How does seeing this map help you better understand why the octopus is not endangered?

Octopus Dangers

Fishers hunt octopuses. They are a common food in Mediterranean and Asian coastal communities. Despite being widely hunted, it is believed octopuses are not endangered. With their wide habitat range and many hiding places, it is hard for scientists to understand the status of octopus populations. The challenge for scientists is estimating octopus population size. Since most octopuses only live one year, scientists rely on newborn octopuses for research. However, the number of young octopus changes from year to year.

Scientists believe octopus populations do not require protection. It is hard for fishers to catch mass amounts of octopus. This is because octopuses usually live alone. One species could face trouble. The mimic octopus is one newly researched octopus. This species is in high demand by zoos since it is newly discovered. But the mimic octopus generally does not survive the move to the aquarium.

The main dangers for octopuses are natural predators. Sharks, moray

Octopus Hunting

Octopus is not very popular on menus in the United States. But in countries such as Italy, Spain, and Vietnam, octopus is a very popular food. The classic method for catching octopuses is to leave empty pots or tin cans attached to strings in the water. Octopuses use these small containers as shelter. When fishers come back to pull up their pots, they pull the octopuses up too.

eels, and dolphins are just some predators. But octopuses are very clever at escaping from predators.

Protecting Themselves

Octopuses have several methods of protecting themselves. Their best defense is to blend in with their surroundings. Octopuses can change shape, color, and texture to not be seen by predators. Their skin has small sacs of yellow, red, black, and brown pigment. This pigment allows octopuses to mimic the patterns in the sand or rock around them.

Master of Mimicry

The mimic octopus is a master at hiding from predators. It can change texture, color, and shape in seconds. But it can also take on the behaviors of some of the ocean's deadliest creatures. When a mimic octopus swims in open water, it can take on the appearance of a lionfish. The lionfish has venom-tipped spikes to warn other animals to stay away. The mimic octopus can also flatten itself out to look like a flounder fish. If in danger, the octopus can mimic the appearance of the sea snake. This is one of the deadliest creatures on Earth.

The mimic octopus was first identified in Indonesia in the early 1990s.

Octopuses can completely camouflage themselves. They can also change texture to blend in even more. When octopuses contract and relax the muscles along their skin, it pinches and pulls their flesh. This makes their skin appear rougher or smoother than normal. Octopuses also use their camouflage talent to sneak up on prey.

Shooting ink is one trick octopuses use to escape predators.

If a hiding place is nearby, an octopus may push itself in there instead. Octopuses can move into tiny cracks because of their super-soft bodies.

If those tricks do not work, and a predator sees the octopus, it may use its inking defense. Octopuses have a sac of black or brown liquid stored in its mantle. When in danger, it can shoot a cloud of ink through its funnel and jet away.

Researchers have been interested in octopus for centuries. Charles Darwin first wrote about octopuses in the early 1800s in his book *The Voyage of the Beagle*:

> *I was much interested, on several occasions, by watching the habits of an Octopus . . . these animals were not easily caught. By means of their long arms and suckers, they could drag their bodies into very narrow crevices; and when thus fixed, it required great force to remove them. At other times they darted tail first, with the rapidity of an arrow, from one side of the pool to the other, at the same instant discolouring the water with a dark chestnut-brown ink. These animals also escape detection by a very extraordinary, chameleon-like power of changing their colour. They appear to vary their tints according to the nature of the ground over which they pass.*

Source: *Charles Darwin.* The Voyage of the Beagle. *New York: Penguin Classics, 1989. Print. 4.*

Nice View

Take a look at Darwin's words. His work is nonfiction. Compare Darwin's information with John Blaine's fiction story in Chapter Three. Think about both authors' points of view. Write a short essay explaining each point of view. How are they similar and why? How are they different and why?

OCTOPUS RESEARCH

Scientists are interested in learning more about octopuses and their level of intelligence. Octopuses' ability to camouflage themselves is especially interesting to scientists. This ability is something scientists want to study more.

Designing E-Readers

Pigment-filled sacs change the color of an octopus's skin. But there are other pigment cells that reflect

All octopuses have the ability to camouflage themselves to match their surroundings. This helps keep them safe from predators.

light and give the patterns their depth. These pigment cells and pigment sacs allow octopuses to change color in seconds.

Scientists wonder if there is something to be learned from this quick color change. Scientists are studying the pigment and light reflectors in cephalopod skin to help them better understand color change. Scientists believe there are ways to apply this use of color and light to technology, such as e-readers.

E-readers use light to show words and images on the screens. Engineers hope learning more

The Octopus Project

OCTOPUS is a project funded by the European Commission. Engineers are building a soft-bodied robotic octopus that can move and act like a real octopus. Researchers want to better understand how an octopus brain and its arms work to create future technologies. Engineers want this robot to push into very tight places too. This robot will be helpful in underwater missions to move under debris and into other places divers cannot reach.

about octopuses' ability to quickly change skin colors will help them copy this technology in e-readers. Engineers are creating even better full-color e-reader displays that will mimic an octopus's changing skin.

Eight-Armed Problem Solvers

Scientists also study how octopuses learn. Divers have reported befriending octopuses when they dive repeatedly in the same areas. The octopuses have learned who the divers are. They recognize the divers and come out to greet them.

Octopuses in captivity have learned new tricks. Octopuses are known for their excellent memories. Some octopuses in aquariums have learned to navigate mazes. When octopuses are reintroduced to the same maze, even after several weeks, they can get through it quickly. The octopuses remember there is food hiding at the end.

Wilson Menashi is a volunteer at the New England Aquarium in Boston, Massachusetts. Menashi created a set of puzzle boxes to challenge the aquarium's

Some octopuses are friendly with divers that frequent their home ranges.

octopuses. He put a crab in a clear plastic box with a simple latch. Menashi lets the octopus open the lid and take the crab out first. After putting the crab back in, he locks the box. When the octopus opens the locked box, Menashi makes the challenge harder. He locks the first box inside of another box. Each time the octopus finishes a challenge, Menashi adds to it. Each octopus Menashi has worked with has learned to overcome the challenges. Menashi's work helps aquarium staff and researchers understand octopuses' ability to learn quickly.

With the ability to open locks, change color and texture, and

Smart and Sneaky

At the Shedd Aquarium in Chicago, Illinois, staff members work with Odie the octopus to better understand octopuses. Keepers work with one of Odie's arms at a time. They reward the arm that does the expected behavior, such as touching a specific colored disk. Odie is sneaky though. When the keepers are focused on one arm, Odie sometimes uses another arm to steal food or a toy.

EXPLORE ONLINE

The focus in Chapter Five is on octopus research. The Web site below has even more information about octopus research. As you know, every source is different. How is the information given in the Web site different from the information given in this chapter? What information is the same? How do the two sources present information differently? What can you learn from this Web site?

Octopus Arms
www.mycorelibrary.com/octopuses

remember how to move through mazes, it is no surprise that a two-spotted octopus flooded the Santa Monica Pier Aquarium. These intelligent cephalopods need to be watched and studied. Scientists still have so much to learn about them.

Scientists are hopeful they will discover more about these amazing invertebrates in the future.

FAST FACTS

Common Name: Common octopus

Scientific Name: *Octopus Vulgaris*

Average Size: 12 to 36 inches (30 to 91 cm)

Average Weight: 6 to 22 pounds (3 to 10 kg)

Color: Variable; can change to match surroundings if needed

Average Lifespan: One year

Diet: Crab, clams, lobsters, fish, and other mollusks

Habitat: Oceans; usually rocky coasts, coral reefs, and sandy areas

Threats: Sharks, moray eels, dolphins, fish, birds, and humans

Intelligence Features

- Octopuses are able to solve problems using trial and error.
- Octopuses can change color, shape, and texture to match their surroundings.
- Octopuses have good memories. They can remember people and maze paths.

Why Do I Care?

You may have never thought about the connection between studying animals and creating technology. But in this book you read about octopus-related technology. How does this information connect to your life? How might your life be different if you had one of these robots? Write down two or three ways this technology connects to your life.

You Are There

Chapter Five discusses how scientists work hard to solve problems and create new technologies. Imagine you are a scientist studying octopuses in an aquarium lab. Write 300 words about your experience. How would you test the octopus's intelligence? What conclusions can you draw from your experiment?

Say What?

Learning about octopuses can mean learning a lot of new vocabulary. Find five words in this book that you've never heard before. Use a dictionary to find out what they mean. Using your own ideas, write down the meaning of each word. Then use each word in a sentence.

Tell the Tale

Chapter Five discusses octopus research. Write 200 words that tell the story of inventions related to octopuses. Describe the features of each item. What is it used for? Be sure to set the scene, develop a sequence of events, and offer a conclusion.

GLOSSARY

camouflage
a structural adaptation that allows a species to blend in with its surroundings

cephalopod
class of marine mollusks that includes nautilus, squid, cuttlefish, and octopus

invertebrates
an animal that lacks a backbone

mantle
muscled sac that contains an octopus's digestive and reproductive organs

mimic
imitate the behavior or appearance of something else

mollusk
a spineless animal with a soft body and a hard shell that usually lives in or near water

pigment
natural coloring

plankton
tiny animals and plants that drift or float in oceans and lakes.

receptor
a cell or group of cells that receives stimuli

valve
a device used to control passage of liquid through a pipe or duct

LEARN MORE

Books

Cosgrove, James A., and Neil McDaniel. *Super Suckers*. Portland: Graphic Arts Center, 2009.

Norman, Mark. *The Octopus's Garden: The Secret World Under the Sea*. Normal, IL: Black Dog, 2008.

Swanson, Diane. *Welcome to the World of Octopuses*. Vancouver: Whitecap, 2010.

Web Links

To learn more about octopuses, visit ABDO Publishing Company online at **www.abdopublishing.com**. Web sites about octopuses are featured on our Book Links page. These links are routinely monitored and updated to provide the most current information available.

Visit **www.mycorelibrary.com** for free additional tools for teachers and students.

INDEX

ABOUT THE AUTHOR

Colleen Kessler is passionate about kids, science, and books. Kessler has a bachelor of science in elementary education, a master of gifted education degree, and is the author of books for teachers and kids.